MW01102074

THE STORY OF

MICROSOFT®

STEVEN FERRY

SMART APPLE MEDIA MANKATO MINNESOTA

Published by Smart Apple Media
123 South Broad Street, Mankato, Minnesota 56001

Copyright © 2000 Smart Apple Media.
International copyrights reserved in all countries.
No part of this book may be reproduced in any form without written
permission from the publisher.

Produced by The Creative Spark, San Juan Capistrano, CA
    Editor: Elizabeth Sirimarco
    Designer: Mary Francis-DeMarois
    Art Direction: Robert Court
    Page Layout: Janine Graham

Photo credits: Jay Thomas/International Stock 4; Dorling Kindersley Limited,
London/Corbis 6; Keren Su/AllStock/PNI 7; Bill Pierce/Rainbow/PNI 8; Dennis
Brack/Black Star/PNI 12; Don Foley/National Geographic Society 14; Don
McCoy/Rainbow/PNI 15; Jim Sugar Photography/Corbis 16; UPI/Corbis-
Bettmann 17; ©Photodisc, Inc. 18; Doug Wilson/Black Star/PNI 20; Tony
Freeman/PhotoEdit/PNI 23; Stephen Frisch/Stock, Boston/PNI 24; Matthew
McVay/AllStock/PNI; Peter Tunley/©Corbis 26; Charles Gupton/Stock,
Boston/PNI 28; Ed Eckstein/Corbis 30; Dan Lamont/Corbis 31; Gary
Benson/All Stock/PNI 32; Steven Ferry/Words & Images 33; Microsoft
Corporation 34; Rob Crandall/Stock, Boston Inc./PNI 39; Kevin Fleming/
Corbis 40; ©PhotoDisc, Inc. 41

Library of Congress Cataloging-in-Publication Data

Ferry, Steven, 1953–
     The story of Microsoft / by Steven Ferry.
     p. cm. — (Spirit of success)
     Includes index.
     SUMMARY: Surveys the computer industry and discusses the founding and
development of Microsoft, one of the biggest and most famous companies in
the world.
     ISBN 1-58340-005-2 (alk. paper)
     1. Microsoft Corporation—History—Juvenile literature. 2. Computer
software industry—United States—History—Juvenile literature. [1. Microsoft
Corporation—History. 2. Computer software industry.] I. Title. II. Series.
     HD9696.63.U64 M535 1999
     338.7610053'0973—dc 21

                                                                98-47649

First edition

9   8   7   6   5   4   3   2   1

Table of Contents

Easier and Faster

Microsoft® Corporation is one of the biggest and most famous companies in the world. It has brought the personal **computer,** or PC, into the lives of millions of people around the world. Each year the company strives to introduce new products for the PC that are more affordable or easier to use than those that came before.

The personal computer has become a vital tool for managing information. Microsoft played an important role in its development. Authors write books on computers. Accountants work with numbers on computers. Young people play games and do their homework on computers. Individuals around the world can communicate with each other on computers.

Bookkeepers and scientists once required many days or weeks to calculate numbers with paper and pencil. Now computer users can accomplish calculations in a split second—and the answer is always right, provided the user has entered the data correctly! Before personal computers were developed, an author making changes to a book took weeks to retype the manuscript on a typewriter. Now the author can input changes and reprint the book in a matter of hours.

There is nothing new about finding better ways to handle information. Microsoft, a world leader in the computer industry, has been working on this since 1975. That isn't very long. Human beings have been inventing better ways to handle information for many thousands of years.

Cave people once kept track of information by carving notches on bones and painting images on the walls of their caves. They needed a way to count the days and record stories. Unfortunately, the notches and marks did not allow cave people to record such information accurately.

Progress in handling information happened slowly. In about 4000 B.C., the Egyptians found a new way to work with numbers. They invented a system of counting using the number 10. That was good progress, but it wasn't until

computer

A machine that can store, retrieve, and process information.

about 2,000 years later that multiplication tables were invented. Before multiplication tables, figuring out "12 x 12" meant spending a lot of time counting one by one up to 144. In about 1500 B.C.—3,500 years before Microsoft—mathematicians in India invented the mathematical concept of "zero." Before that, no one knew how to work with zero as a mathematical idea.

Progress was indeed slow, yet sometimes the inventions were brilliant. Around 500 B.C., the Babylonians invented the abacus, a faster and easier way of adding and subtracting. It was the first portable counting tool and is still in use today. In fact, some abacus users are still faster than many people are on their computers!

In 1642, a French mathematician named Blaise Pascal had an idea to make his father's work easier. His father was

Pascal invented a calculator in 1642. A user input the numbers to be calculated with the dials on the front of the machine. The answer appeared in the holes at the top.

The first abacus had ten movable beads, or counters, on a string. The modern abacus has seven counters on a wire, with a dividing bar that separates the top two beads. The two beads above the bar equal five, while those below equal one. Businesspeople in Asia and the Middle East still use the abacus to calculate numbers.

Charles Babbage first described his Analytical Engine in 1833. Although he labored over the machine for almost 40 years, he was never able to design a machine that worked.

a tax collector who spent long hours keeping track of who owed taxes and exactly how much they owed. There were a lot of numbers to calculate. Blaise invented a machine, which he called the Pascaline, that could add and subtract numbers using wheels.

In 1673, the idea of **binary arithmetic** was invented. A German named Gottfried Leibniz showed that every number could be represented using just two mathematical symbols: zero (0) and one (1). He applied binary arithmetic to the Pascaline computing machine to make it work faster and do more. The Leibniz wheel, as it is now called, could do addition, subtraction, multiplication, and division. The amazing thing about Leibniz's invention is that every computer from 1679 until the present has used the binary system.

In the 19th century, Englishman Charles Babbage invented a machine he called the Analytical Engine. It was the world's first fully automatic calculating machine. Babbage's friend, a woman named Augusta Ada, suggested that the Analytical Engine could be programmed using a set of punched cards that stored information with holes punched in precise places. Every time the machine found a hole in a certain place, it stored, calculated, or printed information depending on where the hole was. Augusta Ada was one of the world's first **programmers.** She created the **program** (the holes in the cards) that gave the machine instructions to follow. Unfortunately, Babbage was never able to make the Analytical Engine work.

binary arithmetic

The use of zeros and ones to stand for numbers, letters, and other information.

programmers

Software designers who create computer programs.

program

A series of instructions supplied to a computer so it can complete a task.

The Binary System

Inside a modern computer, information is not processed using the alphabet (A, B, C, and so on), and the computer doesn't use numbers (1, 2, 3, 4, and so on). The computer uses just two symbols: zero (0) and one (1). The electrical circuits inside a computer can be turned on and off like a light. A circuit is either ON, which is one, or it is OFF, which is zero. The circuits are so fast that they can turn on and off in a billionth of a second!

A user turns the current off and on simply by inputting data, usually with a keyboard. The computer interprets the data as strings of zeros and ones. All these digits strung together are like words in a sentence. The computer reads the strings and works accordingly. Here is how a computer counts from zero to five:

$$0000 = \text{zero}$$
$$0001 = \text{one}$$
$$0010 = \text{two}$$
$$0011 = \text{three}$$
$$0100 = \text{four}$$
$$0101 = \text{five}$$

With a string of four digits made up of zeros and ones, 16 possible combinations exist (16 pieces of information): 0000, 0001, 0010, 0011, 0100, 0101, 0110, 0111, 1000, 1001, 1010, 1011, 1100, 1101, 1110, and 1111. Each of these combinations can stand for any piece of information the user chooses. In the example above, they are numbers. They can be letters in the alphabet, too, such as A equals 0000, B equals 0001, and so on. A computer reads the name Jackie as 100100000010101010000100.

This language is called the binary system. The faster a computer can turn ON (one) and OFF (zero), the faster it can read a name, word, or digit. For example, it turns on and off 24 times to read the name Jackie, 100100000010101010000100.

These are strings of four. If a string of six numbers is used, the possible number of combinations is 64. Computers progressed from using strings of eight numbers (eight bits) to 16 bits and today, strings of 32 zeros and ones. That's billions of combinations, and billions of pieces of information that a binary string can give the computer to read.

The Race of
Progress

I t took thousands of years—and a lot of human effort—
to reach the point where there was enough information
available to invent the Analytical Engine. As technology
entered the 20th century, advances began to happen
much more quickly.

In 1939, a physicist from Iowa State College named
John Atanasoff took one of the first steps toward inventing
the modern computer. Atanasoff wanted to solve
complicated equations more quickly. With the help of

a graduate student named Clifford Berry, he used old-fashioned **electronics** and binary arithmetic to build the ABC, or Atanasoff-Berry Computer. The ABC is considered the forerunner of today's complex, modern computers—the first electronic **digital** computer.

In 1943, during World War II, the British developed a machine they named Colossus. They used it to help break Germany's secret codes. Without Colossus to help organize and compute millions of combinations of letters and numbers, the war might have been over before the British could perform all the calculations. Colossus was the right name for this gigantic machine. It filled a room the size of a small warehouse. It also contained more than 2,400 **vacuum tubes.** These glass tubes were vital to the development of early computers like ABC and Colossus. They had no oxygen inside, so electricity could flow through them quickly. The electricity carried information through the computer. Early computers needed a lot of vacuum tubes to manage information.

In 1945, soon after the invention of Colossus, the U.S. Army built ENIAC (Electronic Numeric Integrator and Computer). ENIAC was so fast that it could solve 5,000 addition problems per second. Unfortunately, ENIAC contained 17,468 vacuum tubes, weighed 30 tons (27 metric tons), and was 100 feet long by 10 feet high (30 meters long by 3 meters high). In 1949, *Popular Mechanics* magazine optimistically predicted that one day computers would weigh no more than 1.5 tons.

electronics

The use of very small bits of energy, moving along in a stream of electricity, to carry information.

digital

A way to communicate using binary arithmetic to translate information (such as sound, words, or pictures) into symbols (zeros and ones). In a computer, those symbols are then sent to a screen and converted back into the original information for the user to see.

vacuum tubes

Glass tubes with all the air removed so electricity can flow through them easily to pass information through a system electronically. Vacuum tubes were used as electrical circuits in computers before the development of the silicon chip.

The ABC Computer

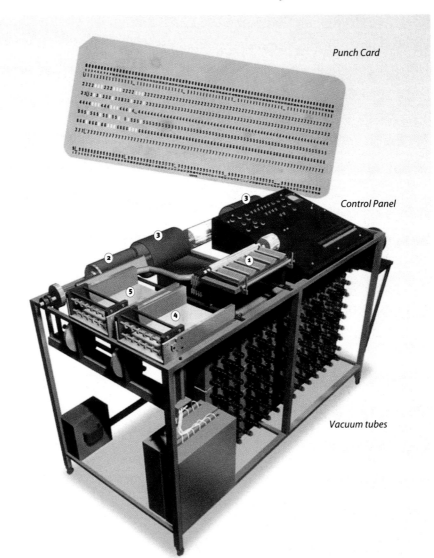

Punch Card

Control Panel

Vacuum tubes

Punch cards, like the one shown above, were inserted into the ABC computer where a device (1) could read and translate the card's information into binary ones and zeros (2). This information was then stored on memory drums (3), recorded on paper (4), and read by electronic readers (5).

Computer scientists decided ENIAC was too big, too slow, and too expensive. By 1960, so-called "mini" computers were made that cost $120,000. By 1962, vacuum tubes were replaced with small wafers made with transistors, the latest electronic technology. This dramatically reduced the size of the newest computers. Just two years later, the cost was down to $18,000, and the mini computer was the size of a refrigerator.

On average, one of ENIAC's vacuum tubes failed every 15 minutes. They were also very hot. In fact, vacuum tubes produce so much heat that ENIAC could now be used to heat New York City!

chips

Tiny pieces of silicon produced to allow electricity, which is carrying information, to flow along a path.

circuit board

The arrangement of circuits, or chips, on a board. Chips are inserted onto circuit boards to transfer information inside a computer.

In 1969, Ted Hoff, a researcher at the Intel® Corporation, invented a way to use tiny **chips** made of silicon. These electrical circuits could contain millions of components but were smaller than a fingernail. He placed the silicon chips on **circuit boards.** Four years later, the first personal computer was born.

In the span of a few years, people had made more progress in information processing than in the thousands of years that came before.

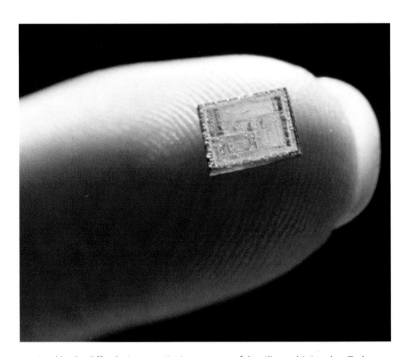

Intel had a difficult time convincing anyone of the silicon chip's value. Today the chip has changed the way people live. Beyond personal computers, chips are found in everything from sprinkler systems to airplanes. The tiny cellular phones so many people carry contain a single chip. If a cellular phone used old-fashioned vacuum tubes instead of the microchip, it would be bigger than the Washington Monument.

The massive ENIAC computer was very different from today's PCs. Tiny chips have replaced vacuum tubes, greatly reducing the size of modern computers.

A Computer on Every Desk

Intel®'s personal computer, with its revolutionary silicon chip and circuit board, had no keyboard or monitor. There were no programs to tell the computer what to do. Nonetheless, people recognized that it had great potential. It could handle all the ones and zeros millions of times faster than the old computers. Unfortunately, there was no way to input data. What Intel's silicon chip and circuit board **hardware** needed was **software.** Computers need software to receive instructions.

All over the world, wherever people were involved in computer technology, programmers started creating software for the new computers. These programmers wrote in code, the **language** based on the binary system that the computer understands.

In 1975, a small company in New Mexico named MITS created the first "micro" computer. It was smaller and faster than the "mini" computer. The inventors called it the Altair. Not only was it smaller and faster, it cost only $350.

At that time, the personal computer was only a metal box with flashing lights and switches. There was still no keyboard or monitor. About the only thing users could do with it was play tic-tac-toe. That didn't stop computer enthusiasts from buying the Altair. MITS took 400 orders for the mini computer in just one afternoon. Within three weeks, the company had earned $250,000.

It was clear that people all around the country were interested in this new technology, but the Altair, like all other computers, needed software. A young man named Bill Gates was a Harvard student at the time. His friend Paul Allen worked for an electronics company called Honeywell. The two men knew that even more people would buy the Altair if it could perform more tasks. They developed a version of the computer programming language known as **BASIC,** which stands for Beginner's All-purpose Symbolic Instruction Code. Gates and Allen's version became known as Altair BASIC.

hardware

The electronic, metal, and plastic parts of the computer as opposed to the software programs that run the computer.

software

The program or operating system that tells the computer's hardware what to do.

language

The codes that computer programmers use to tell a computer what to do.

BASIC

A simple computer language designed in 1963 by two scientists from Dartmouth University. They created BASIC to be a quick and easy programming language for students and beginning computer users.

Microsoft's leader, Bill Gates, started programming computers in the seventh grade at age 13.

The Altair BASIC language worked well. It was efficient and easy for programmers to use. Now the Altair was a real computer, although even with BASIC, it still couldn't do very much.

Altair BASIC was such a good language that Gates and Allen started Microsoft®, a small company dedicated to making software for personal computers. Gates and Allen believed the personal computer would one day be extremely popular in offices and homes. By the end of 1975, Microsoft had earned only $16,000. Microsoft's two founders were sure things would change quickly, however.

In 1976, Altair BASIC caught on with computer enthusiasts. Gates and Allen registered the tradename "Microsoft" with the Secretary of State in New Mexico. The company moved into their first real offices in Albuquerque. In July of that same year, two computer engineers named Steve Wozniak and Steve Jobs introduced the Apple® computer. This new technology came with a keyboard and could be connected to a television monitor. It was much more functional than the Altair. The Apple quickly gained a reputation for being fun and easy to use.

The Apple also needed software. Wozniak and Jobs wanted to include it free of charge with the purchase of their computer. One year later, Microsoft sold the Apple Computer Company a software program called Applesoft BASIC for $21,000. The Apple became enormously popular. The company sold more than one million computers— each one with a copy of Applesoft.

At the end of 1977, Microsoft had nine employees and earned $381,715. A year later, the company earned $1,355,655. Allen and Gates decided it was time to head back to the Pacific Northwest, where they had grown up. In 1979, they moved Microsoft to Bellevue, Washington.

In 1980, Microsoft earned the break Gates and Allen had hoped for. They were asked by International Business Machines (IBM®) to provide the languages and **operating system** software for IBM's first personal computers. Microsoft was now supplying vital software to a worldwide giant in the computer industry. A year later,

Steve Jobs told Microsoft about Apple's new technology, the Macintosh®. Microsoft and Apple decided to team up again. Microsoft became the first major company to develop software for the computer that became known as "the Mac."

Even though computer users loved the Macintosh, IBM was still the largest, most important company in the industry. Other computer makers wanted their machines to be compatible with IBM machines. Since IBM was using Microsoft's software, other companies also chose Microsoft products. By 1982, the company had hired 220 employees to keep up with the increased demand for its products. Microsoft earned nearly $25 million by the end of 1982.

Microsoft products had become well known to everyone in the computer industry. Now Bill Gates and Paul Allen had a decision to make. Should they keep their programming language a secret? If they kept the language exclusively for themselves, they could keep all the money to be earned with it. Companies would have nowhere else to go for their programming.

On the other hand, what if Gates and Allen shared their programming language? Perhaps they could make even more money if the entire computer industry worked together to create products, even if Microsoft's founders would have less control over the right to use their ideas.

Gates and Allen had the vision to make the choice that would help make Microsoft the powerful software company it is today. They decided to create a common

Bill Gates and Paul Allen envisioned a world in which a computer could be found in every office, in every home, and in every classroom all around the world. They hoped that all these computers would run on operating systems created by Microsoft, the company they established in 1975.

operating system that would make all computers speak the same language. They created MS-DOS® (Microsoft Disk Operating System) from a language called Q-DOS that they had purchased from a company called Seattle Computer Products. Then, instead of keeping MS-DOS a secret, Gates and Allen invited other computer programmers to use the system.

Microsoft has sold its products to 180 million people all around the world. Since 1988, the company has been the number-one software vendor in the world.

How important was that decision? Thousands of other software companies have been able to use Microsoft programs to develop their own programs for personal computers. This lowers the cost of software for customers. It also makes a wide range of programs available to the public. Microsoft actually encourages other companies to write programs for Windows® so that its users have a wide variety of software to choose from. The popularity of DOS, and later Windows, has helped make Microsoft the most successful computer company in the world.

Bill Gates in 1983. At age 28, he had already been the chairman of Microsoft Corporation for two years.

Bill Gates: From Programmer to Chairman

William Henry Gates III is the cofounder, chairman, and chief executive officer of Microsoft Corporation. He is one of the most influential people in the computer industry. He may be the wealthiest person in the world.

Bill Gates grew up in Seattle. He was already programming computers in the seventh grade, at age 13. He earned $4,200 one summer for programming class schedules at a neighborhood school. In 1965, he was attending Lakeside School in Seattle. Fourteen-year-old Bill Gates, his good friend Paul Allen, and two other schoolmates formed The Lakeside Programmers Group. Their first real contract was to write a payroll program for a local business.

When Gates was 15, he and Allen started a company called Traf-O-Data. They used a computer to track traffic patterns in Seattle and earned $20,000. When he was 17, Gates took a year off from school to write software programs for a company named TRW. He bought a speedboat with the $30,000 he made that year.

In 1975, while Gates was attending Harvard University, Paul Allen read an article in *Popular Electronics* magazine about a home computer kit— the Altair 8800. Allen and Gates called the owner of Altair. They told him they were working on a computer language based on BASIC. When it was finished, they signed a contract with Altair and were in the computer programming business for good. The two boyhood friends soon formed a partnership they called Microsoft.

Gates, Allen, and Microsoft moved from success to success for many years. Unfortunately, Paul Allen was diagnosed with Hodgkin's disease in 1982. He had to leave Microsoft the following year because of his health. In the years since then, the company has continued to forge ahead.

Many people believe Gates is good for the computer industry, but many others strongly disagree with his views. Whatever people think of him, no one can argue the fact that Gates is one of the most influential people in the personal computer and Internet industries. His views and opinions influence many people because of his knowledge and position within the industry.

"In the personal computer industry," Gates has said, "innovation is the path to success." Innovation means continuing to invent newer, better ways of doing things, and that is the number one goal at Microsoft.

The Fast Lane

No one expected Microsoft® to grow as quickly as it did. In 1986, the company and its 1,153 employees relocated to the town of Redmond, Washington, near Seattle. That same year, Microsoft went public, which means they began to sell **stock** in their company.

Company leaders expected the five buildings at the new Redmond site to provide enough room for at least the next five years. By 1989, however, Microsoft had more than 4,000 employees. The company needed more space again.

Microsoft took over an entire office park, a group of many large buildings that had once been occupied by various different companies. They renamed it Microsoft Place. They even renamed the street where Microsoft is located: The company's official address is "One Microsoft Way."

By 1998, more than 27,000 people worked for Microsoft in 58 countries around the world. More than half of these employees worked at the company's headquarters in Redmond. Microsoft continues to develop improved operating systems, first MS-DOS® and later Windows®. In 1999, the company sold Windows 95, Windows 98, and Windows NT®, which is designed to work on a **network.**

Microsoft Corporation is divided into four main groups. The Sales and Support division sells software and offers technical help. There are different divisions for large organizations, small and medium businesses, schools, and individual computer users.

The Platforms and Applications division employs software engineers who create the different operating systems (platforms) and programs (applications). It develops programs for desktop computers, including Microsoft Office® for businesses, which has more than 23 million users worldwide.

The Interactive Media division develops software for shopping, entertainment, education, and communication over the **Internet.** It produces an on-line magazine called *Slate* that can be accessed on the Internet. It also designs educational CD-ROMs, such as the *Encarta Encyclopedia®*.

stock

Shared ownership in a company by many people who buy shares, or portions, of stock, hoping that the company will make a profit.

network

A group of computers hooked together so they can exchange information. Computers on a network can also share equipment, such as printers and scanners.

Internet

Computers around the world connected into one giant network through which users can communicate.

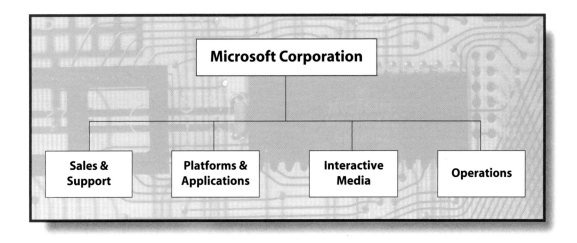

The Interactive Media division teamed up with NBC News to create the 24-hour MSNBC news, talk, and information cable network, as well as a news and information Internet service. Interactive Media also designs computer games such as *3D Movie Maker*® and *Flight Simulator*®.

The Operations division is responsible for giving other companies permission to use Microsoft software. It helps anyone having trouble getting their software to work. Operations also deals with the day-to-day concerns of keeping Microsoft Corporation running smoothly.

As more people use computers, Microsoft keeps growing. To stay so successful, Microsoft works hard to do three things. First of all, it develops new software quickly, allowing users to do more of the things they want to do with their computers. Second, Microsoft makes sure its software is easy to find and sold at reasonable prices.

Windows 95 engineers proudly display their creation on laptop computers. By October 1995, seven million copies of Windows 95 had been purchased. In 1998, Microsoft began selling its updated operating system, Windows 98.

Finally, Microsoft allows other software companies to use its operating system and also provides them with the tools they need to develop new programs.

The result of Microsoft's strategy is that thousands of software companies use Microsoft programs, especially Windows, to develop their own programs. This lowers the cost of software for customers. It also means that a wide range of programs is available to computer users.

Nearly 10,000 employees work in the Research and Development division at Microsoft. Their job is to create new and exciting products for computer users.

Microsoft's Top Products

Microsoft sells hundreds of different software programs that perform many different tasks. Computer users can choose Microsoft products that will help them write a term paper, balance the family budget, or tutor a math student. Children can play with Barney or even visit a three-dimensional island where dinosaurs still live. The company's software engineers spend their workday coming up with new ideas that they think computer users will enjoy.

How Big Is Too Big?

The software industry is growing seven times faster than any other industry in the United States. Competition is fierce. There are thousands of software companies in the world (nine of the 10 largest, including Microsoft®, are U.S. companies). Altogether they sold $253 billion worth of software in 1996.

It takes about 12 to 18 months for most hardware and software to become outdated when faster, more powerful products come along. Software manufacturers must constantly improve their programs in order to stay in business. Microsoft increased spending on research and development of new programs from $350 million in 1992 to $2.6 billion in 1997. It spent twice as much as any other company in the computer industry that year. Even when Microsoft introduces its latest program or operating system, it is already working on the next generation— a newer, more powerful version of the product.

This dedication to staying on top has paid off. In many parts of the world, Microsoft's Windows® operating system controls 90 percent of the **market share.** This means that 90 percent of computer users choose the Windows system to operate their personal computers. In recent years, most software companies design the majority of their programs to work with Windows because it enables them to sell more of their products.

Even the popular Macintosh® computer has had a difficult time competing with Windows. Computer users once chose the Macintosh because it was easy to use. The Macintosh operates using the Mac OS® (OS stands for operating system). Microsoft designed Windows using some of the same ideas that made the Macintosh and the Mac OS so popular.

Windows could be used on more than 1,500 different computer models manufactured by hundreds of different companies. Mac OS could only be used on Apple's Macintosh computers. Windows also became as

chief executive officer (CEO)

The person responsible for managing a company and making decisions that help the company make a profit.

easy to use as the Mac. Programmers began to design more software for Windows and less for the Mac OS. Macintosh sales dropped, and Apple® struggled to survive.

In 1997, Microsoft made a $150 million investment in Apple Computer. Many believe this saved Apple from going out of business. Bill Gates and Steve Jobs, Apple's **chief executive officer (CEO),** announced a partnership between the two companies. They planned to produce versions of Microsoft Office®, Internet Explorer®, and other Microsoft tools for the Mac OS. While this may have saved Apple Computer, critics say that Microsoft's generosity was motivated by its desire to have complete control of the industry.

Now that Microsoft has conquered the PC industry, the company has set its sights on a new frontier: the Internet. In 1995, Gates wrote a best-selling book called *The Road Ahead* in which he explains how important he believes computers will be in the future. Of particular importance, according to Gates, is the Internet.

Computer users now take the Internet and its many uses for granted. Students can research term papers from their desks at home instead of making a trip to the library. International corporations save time and money by communicating with partners across the country and around the world using e-mail. Travelers can check the weather at almost any destination in the world. Media services such as *The New York Times* and the Associated Press can pass on the latest news in a matter of moments. Companies advertise their products on Web sites.

Consumers purchase everything from books and compact discs to clothing and airline tickets using the Internet.

In 1998, there were approximately 57 million people using the Internet in the United States alone. An estimated 133 million users logged on to "the net" worldwide. In that same year, Internet "surfers" had an estimated 320 million Web sites they could visit. Gates believes people will continue to find exciting new ways to utilize the Internet. Microsoft plans to play an important role in the Internet revolution.

Gates himself has said that among the company's biggest goals for the new millennium is to make the Internet easy for everyone to use. "Our framework for this is what I call the Web lifestyle," Gates said in 1998. "This is the idea that over the next decade most adults will be using the Web many times a day, without even thinking about it. Now, to make this happen, we're going to have to dramatically improve the technology."

Microsoft's efforts to sell software for the Internet spurred one of the biggest lawsuits in the history of American business. In October 1998, the United States Department of Justice took Microsoft to federal court. It believed Microsoft had broken the **antitrust laws** that make sure small companies have a fair chance to compete in business against giant corporations.

In 1996, computer manufacturers sold more than 1,500 new models of computers that ran using the Windows operating system. In its Windows 98 operating

antitrust laws

Legislation enacted to protect businesses from unfair practices and monopolies. A monopoly is a situation in which one large company has too much control over an industry.

Internet
browser

A software program
used to access
the Internet.

system, Microsoft included an **Internet browser** called
Microsoft Internet Explorer. This browser automatically
came with any computer that ran on the Windows
operating system.

The U.S. Department of Justice believed that Microsoft
was trying to force other browser companies out of the
market. Smaller companies, such as Netscape®, simply could
not compete for Internet browser business if Microsoft's
product was sold with so many computers. The Justice
Department also claimed that Microsoft used its power to
force Internet service providers and other companies into
exclusive deals using Internet Explorer. This would mean
that such companies could use no other browsers.

Microsoft claimed it planned to include Internet
Explorer as part of Windows 98 before Netscape and other
companies were even founded. The company officials said
computer manufacturers included Internet Explorer on
their systems because it was a good browser program, not
because Microsoft forced them to do so. Competitors
claimed that Microsoft had no interest in the Internet until
it saw the success of companies such as Netscape.

From the beginning, Microsoft had played an
important role in the personal computer revolution. The
U.S. government and competitive computer companies
believed Microsoft's role may have become too important.
They said it used its power to eliminate competition.
Bill Gates defended Microsoft by saying the company
was being punished for its success.

The CEO of Netscape Communications Corporation, James Barksdale, testifies against Microsoft. Bill Gates and Microsoft officials said they first made plans to include an Internet browser with the Windows operating system as early as 1994. Competitors claimed it was eight months after Netscape's popular browser first went on the market that Microsoft began to develop its own technology.

Internet cafes allow users to surf the Web while they enjoy a cup of coffee or lunch. Users can read their e-mail, check out the weather forecast, or even buy a new book in a few moments. Just as Bill Gates predicted, the Internet has become an important part of modern life.

In 1998, Microsoft leaders said that complaints about the company's business practices almost always came from its competitors, not its customers. Computer users have made the company a success because they want quality products and innovative ideas at affordable prices—and Microsoft delivers. Today Microsoft has the resources and the reputation to attract the best computer engineers who can design the most efficient products. This benefits the customer. As long as Microsoft introduces exciting new products that consumers want to buy, the company will remain a driving force in the computer world.

Giving Something Back

Bill Gates and Paul Allen never forgot the Lakeside School, which offered them their first job as computer programmers in 1968. As soon as Microsoft had earned enough money, they contributed more than $2 million to the school for a new science and math building.

Gates continues to give some of his fortune to worthy causes. Over the years, he has donated about $800 million to various charities, including $200 million to the Gates Library Foundation. He founded this organization to help North American libraries purchase computer equipment and software.

Gates also donated all proceeds from the second edition of his popular book, *The Road Ahead*, to schools worldwide. Teachers could use the money to buy computers for their classrooms. "I really owe my success to several excellent teachers," Gates has said, "who gave me the self-confidence when I was very young to explore the world of knowledge." Gates now helps schools in the United States and all around the world.

The Microsoft Corporation does its part as well. The company donates equipment to the same libraries that receive funds from the Gates Library Foundation. A program called Open Studio trains artists to use the Internet to display their work, creating a "virtual art gallery" for people all over the world to enjoy. Microsoft employees sign up for volunteer programs that benefit many different causes in the Seattle area.

Important Moments

1975
MITS promotes Altair BASIC, a program written by Paul Allen and Bill Gates for the first computer designed for consumers.

1978
Microsoft sales exceed $1 million. Microsoft begins to market its software in Japan.

1979
Microsoft markets its products in Europe.

1981
The IBM personal computer and MS-DOS debut.

1983
The Microsoft Word word-processing program is introduced.

1984
Microsoft produces software for the Apple Macintosh computer.

1985
Microsoft introduces the Windows operating system.

1986
Microsoft goes public and moves to Redmond, Washington.

1987
Microsoft offers 10 reference books on CD-ROM, making CD-ROM technology useful for PC users for the first time.

1989
Microsoft becomes the world's number one software vendor.

1990
Microsoft sales exceed $1 billion. Windows 3.0 is introduced.

1991
Microsoft ships four million copies of Windows 3.0 to 24 countries in 12 different languages.

1994
Seven million units of Microsoft Office, a package of several software programs, are sold.

1995
Windows 95 is available. One million copies are sold in the first four days.

1996
Microsoft creates its Interactive Media division and defines its Internet strategy.

1997
Microsoft invests $150 million in Apple Computers. The U.S. Department of Justice files an antitrust complaint against Microsoft.

1998
Microsoft releases Windows 98.

Glossary

antitrust laws
Legislation enacted to protect businesses from unfair practices and monopolies. A monopoly is a situation in which one large company has too much control over an industry.

BASIC
A simple computer language designed in 1963 by two scientists from Dartmouth University. They created BASIC to be a quick and easy programming language for students and beginning computer users.

binary arithmetic
The use of zeros and ones to stand for numbers, letters, and other information.

chief executive officer (CEO)
The person responsible for managing a company and making decisions that help the company make a profit.

chips
Tiny pieces of silicon produced to allow electricity, which is carrying information, to flow along a path.

circuit board
The arrangement of circuits, or chips, on a board. Chips are inserted onto circuit boards to transfer information inside a computer.

computer
A machine that can store, retrieve, and process information.

digital
A way to communicate using binary arithmetic to translate information (such as sound, words, or pictures) into symbols (zeros and ones). In a computer, those symbols are then sent to a screen and converted back into the original information for the user to see.

electronics
The use of very small bits of energy, moving along in a stream of electricity, to carry information.

hardware
The electronic, metal, and plastic parts of the computer as opposed to the software programs that run the computer.

Internet Computers around the world connected into one giant network through which users can communicate.

Internet browser A software program used to access the Internet.

language The codes that computer programmers use to tell a computer what to do. Operating systems and software are both created with computer languages.

market share A product's share of the total sales within a given market.

network A group of computers hooked together so they can exchange information. Computers on a network can also share equipment, such as printers and scanners.

operating system The basic software that allows a computer to communicate and remember information. An operating system also allows other application programs to work together.

program A series of instructions supplied to a computer so it can complete a task.

programmers Software designers who create computer programs.

software The program or operating system that tells a computer's hardware what to do.

stock Shared ownership in a company by many people who buy shares, or portions, of stock, hoping that the company will make a profit.

vacuum tubes Glass tubes with all the air removed so electricity can flow through them easily in order to pass information through a system electronically. Vacuum tubes were used as electrical circuits in computers before the development of the silicon chip.

Index

Items in bold print indicate illustration.

Further Information

Books:

Ichbiah, Daniel and Susan L. Knepper. *The Making of Microsoft.* Rocklin, CA:
Prima Publishers, 1992.

Ken Leebow. *300 Incredible Things for Kids on the Internet.* Colorado Springs, CO:
VIP Publishers, 1998.

Simon, Charman. *Bill Gates: Helping People Use Computers.* Danbury, CT:
Children's Press, 1997.

Web sites:

Microsoft Corporation Web site: http://www.microsoft.com

For more information on the history of computing:
The Virtual Computer History Museum
http://video.cs.vt.edu:90/history

Computer History and Folklore
http://yoyo.cc.monash.edu.au/~mist/Folklore

		DATE DUE	